RACIAL JUSTICE IN AMERI

AAPI HISTORIES

COLONIZATION OF HAWAI'I

VIRGINIA LOH-HAGAN

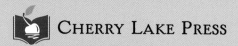
CHERRY LAKE PRESS

Published in the United States of America by Cherry Lake Publishing Group
Ann Arbor, Michigan
www.cherrylakepublishing.com

Reading Adviser: Beth Walker Gambro, MS, Ed., Reading Consultant, Yorkville, IL
Book Design and Cover Art: Felicia Macheske

Photo Credits: © Janis Apels/Shutterstock, 5; © Kues/Shutterstock, 7; © Brandon Bourdages/Shutterstock, 9; © Theodore Trimmer/Shutterstock, 11; Hawai'i State Archives, Photograph Collection, PPWD-16-4, 12; U.S. National Archives, U.S. Senate. Committee on Foreign Relations, Identifier: 595390, 12; © YegoroV/Shutterstock, 15; U.S. National Archives, War Department. Army Air Forces, Identifier: 523939159, 16; © Yanik Chauvin/Shutterstock, 19; © thecolorpixels.com/Shutterstock, 21; © Everett Collection Inc/Alamy Stock Photo, 23; © Chase Clausen/Shutterstock, 25; © Bob Pool, 27; © myboys.me, 28

Graphics Throughout: © debra hughes/Shutterstock.com

Cherry Lake Press is an imprint of Cherry Lake Publishing Group.

Library of Congress Cataloging-in-Publication Data

Names: Loh-Hagan, Virginia, author.
Title: Colonization of Hawai'i / by Virginia Loh-Hagan.
Description: Ann Arbor, Michigan : Cherry Lake Publishing, [2022]
  | Series: Racial justice in America : AAPI histories | Includes bibliographical
  references. | Audience: Grades 4-6
Identifiers: LCCN 2022005362 | ISBN 9781668909317 (hardcover)
  | ISBN 9781668910917 (paperback) | ISBN 9781668914090 (pdf)
  | ISBN 9781668912508 (ebook)
Subjects: LCSH: Hawaiians—Colonization—Juvenile literature. |
  Hawaiians—Social conditions—Juvenile literature. |
  Hawaii—History—Juvenile literature. | Decolonization—Hawaii—Juvenile
  literature.
Classification: LCC DU625 .L85 2022 | DDC 996.9—dc23/eng/20220208
LC record available at https://lccn.loc.gov/2022005362

Cherry Lake Publishing Group would like to acknowledge the work of the Partnership for 21st Century Learning, a Network of Battelle for Kids. Please visit *http://www.battelleforkids.org/networks/p21* for more information.

Printed in the United States of America

Dr. Virginia Loh-Hagan is an author, former K-8 teacher, curriculum designer, and university professor. She's currently the Director of the Asian Pacific Islander Desi American (APIDA) Center at San Diego State University. She is also the Co-Executive Director of the Asian American Education Project. She identifies as Chinese American and is committed to amplifying APIDA communities.

CHAPTER 1

What Does Decolonization Mean?

Imagine the place where you live is being invaded. Your rights are taken away. Your lands are seized. You're forced to speak another language. Your native culture is at risk. That's what happened to Native Hawaiians. Hawai'i is a group of islands in the Pacific Ocean. It was once a thriving kingdom. Then the United States colonized it and later made it into a state. The U.S. government took over and exploited Hawaiian lands and resources. It forced American culture on Native Hawaiians. Native Hawaiians continue to fight for independence. They are actively working to reclaim what has been lost.

It's important to "decolonize" how we think about Hawai'i. We need to see Hawai'i as more than a tourist hotspot. We need to understand its history and honor its culture. Because of the United States, Hawai'i has been negatively changed in many ways. We need to be critical of the role the United States played in colonizing Hawai'i.

A big part of decolonization is centering Native people's narratives. This means understanding Hawai'i from the perspectives of Native Hawaiians. It also means challenging systems that oppress others.

Hawai'i is about 2,000 miles (3,219 kilometers) from the U.S. mainland.

The word *Hawaii* is product of colonization. It is used to describe the state of Hawaii. This is how the U.S. government spelled and pronounced it. This spelling should remind us of the state's colonized history. On the other hand, Native Hawaiians use "Hawai'i." The little mark is called an *'okina*. It looks like a backward apostrophe. But it's not a punctuation mark. It's an actual letter in the Hawaiian language. It represents a glottal stop, which is a break between vowels.

Hawai'i is derived from the name of its largest island, Hawai'i. According to a native legend, it is named for a fisherman, Hawai'iloa. He was famous for taking long fishing trips. On one of his trips, he discovered Hawai'i. He returned to the island with his family and settled there. His children were Maui, Kaua'i, and O'ahu. They settled on the islands that bear their names.

Think About It! Hawai'i is the only state with an Asian American majority. Honolulu has more Asian Americans than any other U.S. city. Research the immigration of Asian Americans. Why are there more Asian Americans in Hawai'i?

The 'okina changes the pronunciation and meaning of a word. For example, kou means "yours." Ko'u, with an 'okina, means "mine."

DID YOU KNOW...?

The traditional name of the Native Hawaiian people is Kānaka Maoli. It means "true human beings." The Kānaka Maoli make up about 20 percent of the state's population. Some experts think there are only about 5,000 Kānaka Maoli left. The Kānaka Maoli have a deep love of the land. This love is called 'Aina. 'Aina refers to Hawai'i and its natural resources. The Kānaka Maoli believe they are stewards of the land. Their job is to take care of the land. They do this for future generations.

CHAPTER 2

What Is the History of the Colonization of Hawai'i?

Polynesians from the Marquesas Islands were the first to settle in Hawai'i. They traveled in canoes. They were expert farmers and fishermen. They lived in small communities ruled by chiefs. They created strong trade networks.

In 1778, British explorer Captain James Cook landed on Kaua'i. Cook and his crew became the first Europeans to reach the Hawaiian islands. He named the islands after his **patron**, John Montague, who was the Earl of Sandwich. As colonizers, they called Hawai'i the Sandwich Islands. They exploited the Native people by taking their resources. They also brought diseases to the islands. Many Native Hawaiians died.

In 1779, Cook visited Hawai'i for the third time. Tensions grew between the Europeans and Native Hawaiians. Cook had taken sacred wood from a burial site. He had also kidnapped one of the chiefs for stealing his boat. This angered the Native Hawaiians. A fight broke out and Cook was killed. Several Native Hawaiians died as well.

Before he died, Cook wrote about his voyages. This attracted European and American explorers, traders, and whalers. They used Hawai'i as a rest stop for supplies.

The flag of the state of Hawai'i has the British flag in the corner. It is the only U.S. state flag to include a foreign country's national flag.

The more popular Hawai'i became, the more it was colonized. By 1820, American groups converted Native Hawaiians to Christianity. They also established schools on the islands. This resulted in the erasing of native culture. By 1835, wealthy American and European businessmen started the first sugarcane plantations. They profited greatly from Hawaiian resources.

Between 1791 and 1810, King Kamehameha I conquered other Hawaiian chiefs. He united the islands into the kingdom of Hawai'i. The kingdom was known around the world as an independent nation. Yet, by 1887, Americans and Europeans had gained a lot of power in Hawai'i. They passed laws that benefited them. They pushed through the Bayonet Constitution. King Kalākaua, a descendant of Kamehamaeha, was forced to sign this this law at gunpoint. This law stripped away the monarchy's power. It gave the right to vote to rich landowners. This excluded Native Hawaiians and workers from other countries. Only White residents were allowed to vote.

Think About It! The Philippines became a U.S. territory in 1898. It gained independence in 1946. Learn more about this history. How did Filipinos feel about being a territory? How did the United States benefit? How did the Filipinos benefit? How did they suffer?

King Kamehameha, the first king of Hawai'i, died in 1819. But floral parades are held every June 11 in his honor. This day is known as King Kamehameha Day.

DID YOU KNOW...?

The Hawaiian islands were isolated. This kept them safe from diseases. But when outsiders came, their diseases came with them. Native Hawaiians did not have immunity to fight the diseases. In the late 1800s, leprosy spread and threatened to wipe out the population. The Kingdom of Hawai'i set aside Kalaupapa on the island of Moloka'i as a leper colony. Those with leprosy were forced to live there, far away from others. They were removed from their homes and banished. Today, Kalaupapa is a national park.

Queen Liliʻuokalani was the last Hawaiian ruler. She was held in house arrest at Iolani Palace in Honolulu. Today, it is open to the public for tours.

In 1893, Hawaiʻi was ruled by Queen Liliʻuokalani, a descendant of Kamehameha. Queen Liliʻuokalani wanted to restore power to the monarchy. She also fought to give Native Hawaiians the right to vote. A group of wealthy American businessmen arrested and removed Queen Liliʻuokalani from power. They established their own government with Sanford Dole as its president. President Grover Cleveland ordered the queen to be restored. But Dole refused.

In 1898, the Spanish-American War began. The United States fought against Spanish colonial rule in the Philippines. It wanted to gain more territories in the Pacific. This made Hawaiʻi useful as a naval base. That year, the United States annexed Hawaiʻi as a territory.

To stop Hawaiʻi from gaining independence, the U.S. government organized a vote to make Hawaiʻi a state. White settlers and military members outnumbered Native Hawaiians. They voted for statehood. The islands became the 50th state in 1959. Many Native Hawaiians disputed the vote because there were only two options. One option was to stay a U.S. territory. The other option was to become a state. There was no option for independence.

CHAPTER 3

Why Did The United States Want To Colonize Hawai'i?

In the 1840s, the United States believed in Manifest Destiny. This was a belief in the country's God-given right to expand its borders in the name of liberty and freedom. The United States sought to conquer lands to the Pacific Ocean and beyond. In doing so, it removed Native people from their homes and erased their cultures.

By 1853, the United States had conquered much of the West. It looked to the Pacific to expand. This benefited the United States in many ways. It wanted to increase resources and make money. It also wanted to remain the dominant power in the Pacific.

Businessmen, not the government, pursued manifest destiny in Hawai'i. They took advantage of Native Hawaiians. They made laws that gave them access to Hawaiian land. They then took as much land as possible. Native Hawaiians were not familiar with the idea of owning land. They didn't know they needed to make claims for the land on which they lived or worked. By the late 1850s, few Native Hawaiians had made claims. Instead, foreigners owned and controlled almost all the land. The Native Hawaiians, however, still worked the land. The United States exploited both their land and labor.

Think About It! The Native people of Hawai'i are called Hawaiians. However, living in Hawai'i does not make one Hawaiian. It makes one a resident of Hawai'i. Whereas, living in New York makes one a New Yorker. What does this mean? How is Hawai'i different from other states?

Breakdown of volcanic material forms fertile soil over thousands of years. Hawai'i has rich soils that are great for growing sugar, pineapple, coffee, nuts, and more.

The U.S. Pacific Fleet's main purpose was to stop Japan from expanding and colonizing.

DID YOU KNOW...?

The media plays a big role in shaping public opinion. It can affect how people see colonization. The overthrow of Queen Lili'uokalani was unfairly portrayed. American newspapers and magazines published political cartoons about her. In these cartoons, Queen Lili'uokalani was drawn as an uncivilized savage. This helped to justify U.S. actions. In reality, Queen Lili'uokalani ruled over a highly civilized nation. She lived in a Victorian-style palace. Her palace was one of the first to have electricity and indoor toilets. She was accepted as a ruler by many European rulers. She was a talented musician. She was far from being a so-called savage.

A 1875 law allowed Hawai'i to sell sugar without paying taxes. U.S. business owners made a lot of money from sugar plantations. They made up less than 10 percent of the population. But they owned most of the wealth. An 1890 law increased the taxes on foreign sugar growers. Businessmen in Hawai'i didn't want to pay the high taxes. They pushed to make Hawai'i a territory and a state. They did this so their sugar wouldn't be taxed as a foreign product.

Another way the United States profits from colonizing Hawai'i is through tourism. Statehood allowed for Hawai'i to become a tourist attraction. The state attracts tourists, surfers, and scientists from around the world. Hawai'i is known for its warm weather, striking beaches, and lush land. Tourism generates billions of dollars.

During the 1890s, the United States wanted to improve its economy. It needed to open international markets. To do this, it needed ships. The U.S. government wanted exclusive rights to use Pearl Harbor in Hawai'i. Pearl Harbor was a key location. It was one of the largest natural harbors in the Pacific Ocean. Today, Pearl Harbor hosts the U.S. Pacific Fleet, the world's largest naval command.

CHAPTER 4

What Are the Effects of Colonization on Hawai'i?

The United States does not see itself as a conqueror. This is because of **American exceptionalism**. The United States believed it was special. It believed it was spreading liberty and freedom. By taking over other countries, it thought it was saving the Native people. This thinking was used to justify colonization and **imperialism**.

Native Hawaiians did not need to be saved. They were thriving before contact with Europeans and Americans. Europeans and Americans brought deadly diseases. They also brought **poverty** by taking Hawaiian resources for themselves.

In addition, the United States actively erased **native knowledge** and culture. American culture was seen as superior to Hawaiian culture. For example, in 1896, the

United States banned Native Hawaiians from speaking their own language. Schools were set up to Americanize Hawaiian children, or make them more American. Children speaking Hawaiian were punished.

Today, many Native Hawaiians can't speak Hawaiian fluently. But activists have been working to change this. In 1978, the Hawaiian language was reinstated as the official language of the state. Hawaiian language schools have been established. Some Hawaiians are relearning their native language.

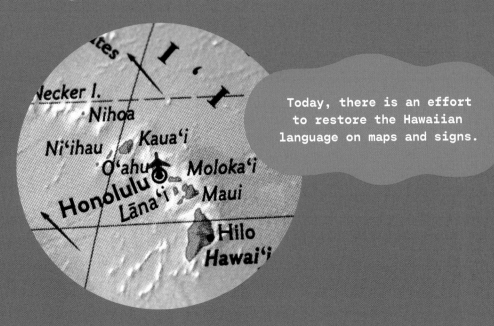

Today, there is an effort to restore the Hawaiian language on maps and signs.

Think About It! People of color suffer more health problems due to racist laws and practices. This is called environmental racism. Learn more about it. How does what is happening in Hawai'i an example of environmental racism?

The United States also disrupted the Hawaiian way of life. Native Hawaiians believe in "malama ka 'aina." This means to care for the land, so it supports future generations. In the past, Native Hawaiians had native knowledge. They lived as one with the natural world. They farmed and hunted only what they needed. On the other hand, the United States had a different view. They saw natural resources as goods to be bought and sold. Because of colonization, much native knowledge is lost. Today, Native Hawaiians are learning to be reconnected to the land.

Colonizing Hawai'i also negatively impacted its environment. Tourism brought in mass development. Hawaiian communities were destroyed by the building of hotels, resorts, and roads. Businessmen even destroyed ancient burial sites. These changes were all made for the purpose of entertaining tourists.

All this building increased land, air, and water pollution. It also caused habitat loss. Many animals and plants have died out and are now extinct. Native Hawaiians have also been displaced. The large military presence in Hawai'i forced many Native people from their homelands.

Native Hawaiians have specific names for different rains and winds. This shows a deep knowledge of nature.

DID YOU KNOW...?

Larry Kimura is a professor at the University of Hawai'i at Hilo. He is called the "grandfather" of the Hawaiian language revitalization movement. In the 1980s, he helped start the first Hawaiian language preschools. He also started a radio program where he interviewed Native Hawaiian speakers. He believes people want to connect with their elders. He wants to save the Hawaiian language from being lost. He said, "Language is the first aspect of a people to vanish." He's committed to creating a new generation of Hawaiian language speakers. His dream is to hear Hawaiian spoken everywhere in Hawai'i.

CHAPTER 5

What Is the Hawaiian Sovereignty Movement?

The Hawaiian **sovereignty** movement is a fight for independence. This fight started after Queen Liliʻuokalani was overthrown. Sovereignty activists argue her ousting was illegal. They accuse the United States of stealing their lands. They point to colonization as the source of their problems. They are seeking **self-determination** and **self-governance**. They want to be able to determine how they are to be governed. They want control over their lands and lives.

Efforts to legally reclaim Hawaiian lands have been unhelpful. In 1893, U.S. President Grover Cleveland ordered an investigation. The investigation found the removal of Queen Liliʻuokalani to be illegal. But in 1894, another investigation said the opposite. In 1993, U.S. President Bill Clinton issued an apology. He acknowledged that the Hawaiian people never gave their lands to the United States. He also admitted that the United States was at fault for providing military support to overthrow Queen Liliʻuokalani. However, in 2009, the U.S. Supreme Court ruled that the apology had no power to return lands.

During World War II (1939–1945), Hawaiʻi was under martial law. Martial law is when the military rules the land. The United States took thousands of acres of land during this time.

Native Hawaiians hosted their own investigation. In 1993, the Peoples' International Tribunal was formed. Leaders of native cultures from around the world served as judges. They traveled to five Hawaiian islands. They listened to testimonies from many Native Hawaiians. They found the United States to be guilty of crimes against Native Hawaiians. The tribunal asked for the United States to restore and return all lands to Native Hawaiians.

Many groups are fighting for Hawaiian sovereignty. There are two main perspectives. Some groups want restoration. They want the United States to give back lands. They want to separate from the United States. They want to be an independent nation.

Other groups want federal recognition. They think restoration will never happen. Instead, they want tribal status. They want to have the same rights as Native Americans. They want to have control over some of their lands. They want to be a nation within a nation.

Think About It! Houses in Hawai'i are very expensive. Many Native Hawaiians can't afford to buy a house in their own homelands. Why is this a problem?

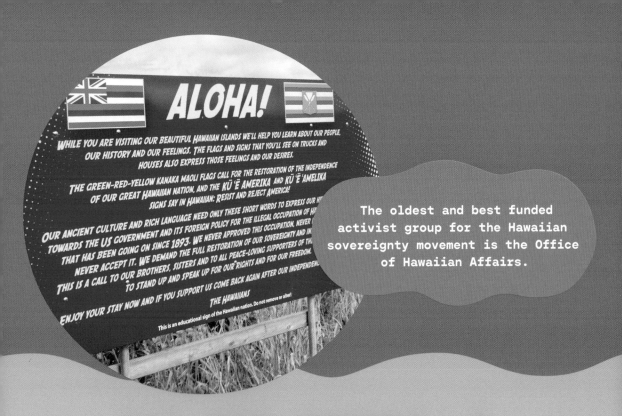

ALOHA!

WHILE YOU ARE VISITING OUR BEAUTIFUL HAWAIIAN ISLANDS WE'LL HELP YOU LEARN ABOUT OUR PEOPLE, OUR HISTORY AND OUR FEELINGS. THE FLAGS AND SIGNS THAT YOU'LL SEE ON TRUCKS AND HOUSES ALSO EXPRESS THOSE FEELINGS AND OUR DESIRES.

THE GREEN-RED-YELLOW KANAKA MAOLI FLAGS CALL FOR THE RESTORATION OF THE INDEPENDENCE OF OUR GREAT HAWAIIAN NATION, AND THE KŪ'Ē AMERIKA AND KŪ'Ē 'AMELIKĀ SIGNS SAY IN HAWAIIAN: RESIST AND REJECT AMERICA!

OUR ANCIENT CULTURE AND RICH LANGUAGE NEED ONLY THESE SHORT WORDS TO EXPRESS OUR H[...] TOWARDS THE US GOVERNMENT AND ITS FOREIGN POLICY FOR THE ILLEGAL OCCUPATION OF HA[...] THAT HAS BEEN GOING ON SINCE 1893. WE NEVER APPROVED THIS OCCUPATION, NEVER [...] NEVER ACCEPT IT. WE DEMAND THE FULL RESTORATION OF OUR SOVEREIGNTY AND IN[...] THIS IS A CALL TO OUR BROTHERS, SISTERS AND TO ALL PEACE-LOVING SUPPORTERS OF TH[...] TO STAND UP AND SPEAK UP FOR OUR RIGHTS AND FOR OUR FREEDOM.

ENJOY YOUR STAY NOW AND IF YOU SUPPORT US COME BACK AGAIN AFTER OUR INDEPENDEN[...]

THE HAWAIIANS

This is an educational sign of the Hawaiian nation. Do not remove or alter!

The oldest and best funded activist group for the Hawaiian sovereignty movement is the Office of Hawaiian Affairs.

DID YOU KNOW...?

Many examples of Hawaiian resistance to U.S. rule exist. For example, the Kalama Valley protests took place in 1971. Native Hawaiian farmers were living in Kalama Valley. They were evicted, or forced out, from their lands. American businessmen wanted the lands to build a resort. They started to demolish buildings. Some families refused to leave. Protests and rallies were organized. More evictions in surrounding lands took place. Activists accused the United States of removing Native Hawaiians from their own lands. They said the evictions were illegal. The Kalama Valley protests sparked discussions about land rights and struggles between locals, businessmen, and tourists.

CHAPTER 6

What Else Is Still Happening Today?

Hawai'i is still being exploited for its land. Mauna Kea is a dormant volcano. To Native Hawaiians, it's their most sacred site. In Ancient Hawaiian times, only chiefs were allowed to visit it. A Native Hawaiian said, "It's a place where humans don't belong, where gods reside."

Mauna Kea is the highest point in the state. It is dry and has a stable airflow. This makes it an ideal site to observe space. Several nations want to build the Thirty Meter Telescope (TMT) on Mauna Kea. The TMT would be the largest telescope in the northern part of the world.

Native Hawaiians are protesting this telescope. They have had enough of outsiders using their lands. Starting in 2014, they blocked roads. This action stopped construction crews from working. Protestors camped on the road. They rolled large rocks onto the roads. They did whatever they could to stop crews from working. Many were arrested. People from around the world have come to support them. These protests are bringing Hawaiian land rights into national conversations.

When Europeans came, they introduced cattle and sheep. These animals damaged Mauna Kea's ecosystem.

Hawai'i was the first in the nation to require travelers to quarantine for 14 days.

Native Hawaiians are still suffering from diseases brought from outsiders. During the COVID-19 pandemic, Native Hawaiians begged tourists to stop visiting. Governor David Ige said, "It is not a good time to travel to the islands. I encourage everyone to restrict and curtail travel to Hawai'i."

Native Hawaiians suffer from a lack of access to healthcare. Hawai'i's hospitals are often full and understaffed. Native Hawaiians have died from COVID-19 at a faster rate than other groups. They account for 40 percent of the state's COVID deaths. Some Native Hawaiians are wary of the COVID vaccine. Given their history, they do not trust the government.

Native Hawaiians have not been well-served by the government. They have lower incomes. They have higher poverty rates. They have higher prison rates. They have higher school dropout rates. They have suffered under a system that has denied them rights and opportunities. This is the legacy of colonization.

Think About It! In 2021, a lion at the Honolulu Zoo died from COVID-19. Learn more about it. What are some other effects of COVID-19? How were you affected by COVID-19?

DID YOU KNOW...?

The Thirty Meter Telescope (TMT) protests have led some people to think Native Hawaiians are opposed to science. They accuse Native Hawaiians of stopping progress. But that is not the case. Native Hawaiians are protecting their lands. They have nothing against science and progress. In fact, Native Hawaiians were among the first to use electricity. King Kalākaua's palace installed electricity before the White House did. Kalākaua showed the world that Hawai'i was a scientific leader. He also adopted other technology, such as running water, flush toilets, and even a phone in his library.

SHOW WHAT YOU KNOW!

A major injustice happened when Hawai'i was colonized. Hawaiian lands were stolen. Their way of life was almost erased. Let's work to never let this happen again.

Learn more about the effects of colonization in Hawai'i. Colonization led to long-lasting impacts. It changed the land and culture, affecting generations. It's important to see things from the perspective of the Hawaiian people. Decolonize your thinking.

Show what you know! Choose one or more of these activities:

- Learn more about Hawaiian concepts. For example, learn what *aloha* really means. It means more than just hello. In Native Hawaiian culture, it means recognizing the breath of life in another human.

- Research Native Hawaiian resistance. Learn about ways the people have protested and fought back. It's important to understand the power that Native Hawaiians had and still have.

- Read all the books in the *Racial Justice in America* series. Create a journal, podcast, or social media campaign. Include a segment about the colonization of Hawai'i.

 Think About It! Think about all the things you have learned. What would you like to learn more about?

SHOW WHAT YOU CAN DO!

Share your learning. Being an ally is the first step in racial justice work. Allies recognize their privilege. We all come from different positions of privilege. We also have different types of privilege. In the United States, being White is a privilege. Other examples include being male or an English speaker.

Use your privilege to help all achieve equality. Learning about the colonization of Hawai'i taught us that the United States committed injustices in the name of progress. Here are ways you can be an ally:

- Encourage people visiting Hawai'i to learn about its colonized history. Teach them to be responsible and respectful visitors.

- Be a steward of the land. Learn ways to better care for the land. Encourage others to do the same.

- Try to pronounce Hawaiian words correctly. Help preserve the language.

We all have a role to play in racial injustice. We also have a role in making a better world. Do your part. Commit to racial justice!

Think About It! Think about your privileges. Do you want to improve the lives of others? What are you willing to give up to do this?

EXTEND YOUR LEARNING

NONFICTION

Loh-Hagan, Virginia. *A is for Asian American: An Asian Pacific Islander Desi American Alphabet Book*. Ann Arbor, MI: Sleeping Bear Press, 2022.

Loomis, Jim. *Fascinating Facts About Hawai'i*. Honolulu, HI: Watermark Publishing, 2019.

Public Broadcasting Service: Asian Americans
https://www.pbs.org/weta/asian-americans

GLOSSARY

ally (AH-lye) a person who is aware of their privilege and supports oppressed communities

American exceptionalism (uh-MER-uh-kuhn ik-SEP-shnuh-lih-zuhm) the idea that the United States has a special mission to bring freedom to all

annexed (AA-nekst) seized and took control of another area or country

Bayonet Constitution (BAY-uh-nuht kahn-stuh-TOO-shuhn) the 1887 agreement the king of Hawai'i was forced to sign at gunpoint; a bayonet is a gun with a long knife attached to the end

colonized (KAH-luh-nyzd) took control of a people or area especially as an extension of state power

decolonize (dee- KAH-luh-nyz) to deconstruct colonial ideas of the superiority and privilege of western culture

descendant (dih-SEHN-duhnt) a member of the future generation of people

federal recognition (FEH-duh-ruhl reh-kihg-NIH-shuhn) having a special legal relationship with the U.S. government

glottal stop (GLAH-tuhl STAHP) a speech sound made by briefly stopping the flow of air through the vocal cords

imperialism (im-PIHR-ee-uh-lih-zuhm) policy of expanding national territory by taking over another country

leprosy (LEH-pruh-see) a serious infectious disease affecting the skin and nervous system

Manifest Destiny (MAH-nuh-fest DEH-stuh-nee) the belief that the United States had a divine mission to expand westward across North America and beyond

monarchy (MAH-nuhr-kee) a form of government ruled by a king or queen

narratives (NER-uh-tivz) stories or perspectives

native (NAY-tiv) having origin in a country or area; the first people to live in an area

native knowledge (NAY-tiv NAH-lij) understandings, skills, and philosophies developed by societies with long histories of interaction with their natural surroundings

pandemic (pan-DEH-mik) an epidemic spread over multiple countries or continents

patron (PAY-truhn) a person who gives generous support or approval

plantations (plan-TAY-shuhnz) large farms or estates used for growing crops to sell

Polynesians (pah-luh-NEE-zhuhnz) people from a large group of islands in the central pacific ocean

poverty (PAH-vuhr-tee) not having enough money for basic needs such as food, water, or shelter

privilege (PRIV-lij) a special, unearned right or advantage given to a chosen person or group

self-determination (SELF di-tuhr-muh-NAY-shuhn) the belief that all people have the right to control their own lives and make choices for their futures

self-governance (SELF GUH-vuhr-nuhns) the belief that all people have the right to rule themselves

sovereignty (SAH-vuh-ruhn-tee) the right of a government to have complete control over its area

territories (TER-uh-tohr-eez) geographical areas belonging to or under the rule of a government

tourism (TUR-ih-zuhm) the process of spending time away from home in pursuit of pleasure or fun while using services such as hotels, restaurants, etc.

tribunal (try-BYOO-nuhl) a court or forum of justice

INDEX